THIS CANDLEWICK BOOK BELONGS TO:

Kay Gelner 6/96

For Beatrice and Olivia

First U.S. edition 1994
First published in Great Britain in 1993 by Walker Books Ltd., London.

Library of Congress Cataloging-in-Publication Data is available.
Library of Congress Catalog Card Number 93-24148

ISBN 1-56402-251-X

10 9 8 7 6 5 4 3 2 1

Printed in Hong Kong

The pictures this book were done in watercolor.

Candlewick Press
2067 Massachusetts Avenue
Cambridge, Massachusetts 02140

TEN LITTLE TEDDIES

Lucy Su

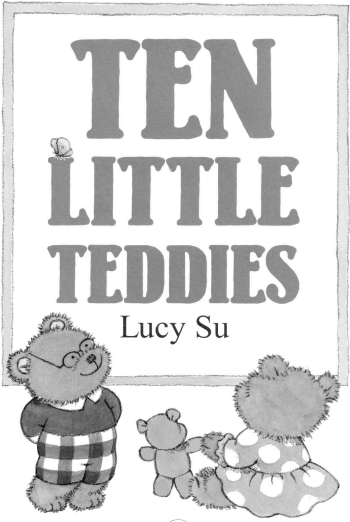

CANDLEWICK PRESS
CAMBRIDGE, MASSACHUSETTS

Ten little teddies are off to the park.

Ten little teddies won't be back till dark.

Ten little teddies run in the sun.

Nine little teddies have lots of fun.

Eight little teddies by the piglets stop.

Seven little teddies watch the rabbits hop.

Six little teddies swing up so high.

Five little teddies watch the ducks go by.

Four little teddies stop to have a rest.

Three little teddies find a blackbird's nest.

Two little teddies make mud pies.

One little teddy chases butterflies.

No little teddies—where can they be found?

Here they all are on the merry-go-round!

LUCY SU was born in 1948, the daughter of an accomplished calligrapher from China. She was inspired to create *Ten Little Teddies* by a small park near her home where she takes her small daughters to play and "rush about."

Other Candlewick books by Lucy Su:

Jinzi and Minzi Are Friends
Jinzi and Minzi at the Playground